G000278575

£7.95

'THE LAST BLACKBIRD'
and other poems by
Ralph Hodgson

Edited and introduced
by John Harding

GREENWICH EXCHANGE
LONDON

Greenwich Exchange, London

First published in Great Britain in 2004
All rights reserved

Ralph Hodgson's poems are printed with the kind permission of
Bryn Mawr College.

Printed and bound by Q3 Digital/Litho, Loughborough
Tel: 01509 213456
Typesetting and layout by Albion Associates, London
Tel: 020 8852 4646
Cover design by December Publications, Belfast
Tel: 028 00286559

Cover picture: Mary Evans Picture Library

Greenwich Exchange Website: www.greenex.co.uk

ISBN 1-871551-81-1

Ralph Hodgson,
his Book.

To Bob and Sybil Hodgson, Betty Beesley and
Shirley Colquhoun

Contents

Chronology

1871	Born in Darlington, County Durham.
1889	Works as a cartoonist in Fleet Street.
1904	First poem published in *Saturday Review.*
1907	First Collection published: *Last Blackbird.*
1911	Edits *New Fry's* magazine.
1913	Flying Fames appear.
1914	Wins Polignac Prize.
1915	Included in *Georgian Poetry II.*
1917	Included in *Georgian Poetry III.*
1917	*Collected Poems* published.
1923-1938	Teaches in Japan.
1939	Moves to USA.
1946	Receives Annual Award of the National Institute of Art and Letters (USA).
1951-1955	'Flying Scrolls' appear.
1954	Wins Queens Gold Medal for Poetry.
1958	'The Skylark' published.
1961	*Collected Poems* published.
1962	Dies in Canton, Ohio, USA.

Introduction

The Poet

> My daughter is heavier. Light leaves are flying.
> Everywhere in enormous numbers turkeys will be dying
>   & other birds, all their wings.
> They never greatly flew. Did they wish to?
> I should know. Off away somewhere once I knew
>   such things.
>
> Or good Ralph Hodgson back then did, or does.
> The man is dead whom Eliot praised. My praise
>   follows & flows too late ...
>
> John Berryman. *The Last Dream Song*: 161 (1965)

The poet and cartoonist Ralph Hodgson was born in Darlington, County Durham, on the 9th September 1871, the sixth son in a family of seven boys and three girls. His father was a coal merchant who died when Ralph was just seven; his mother, Mary, then supported the family by opening a private school. Hodgson's own formal education did not progress much beyond elementary school: he was apt to roam, and spent much of his teens working with travelling fairs and performing in boxing booths.

His principal talent was artistic, however, and in 1889 he found work as a cartoonist on an early children's comic, *Funny Cuts*. In 1893 he was employed by Alfred Harmsworth (later Lord Northcliffe) as the lead cartoonist on the latter's *Evening News*, the first British popular newspaper. Later, he worked on journals such as Jerome K. Jerome's *The Idler* and collaborated with cartoonists/illustrators such as Alfred Sime and Phil May on the *Minster* magazine. In 1897 he returned to children's comics on Arthur Pearson's seminal *Big Budget*. Here Hodgson worked alongside Tom Browne (whom he eventually succeeded as art editor in 1900) and Jack B. Yeats, producing comic strips such as 'Airey Alf and Bouncing Billy'.

It was while working on *Big Budget* that he was persuaded by the playwright Rudolph Besier (of *The Barrett's of Wimpole Street* fame) to submit certain poems to the *Saturday Review*. In November 1904 'The Storm Thrush' appeared, the first of many pieces to be featured in the *Review* in the years leading up to the First World War.

Poetry now became his principal occupation, though his output would always be sparse, his subsequent reputation resting on just two early collections: *The Last Blackbird* (1907) and *Poems* (1917). Two poems from the latter collection helped win him the Polignac Prize in 1914, previously awarded to Walter De La Mare, James Stephens and John Masefield. He was also featured in two volumes of the *Georgian Anthology* (1915 and 1917) series, edited by Edward Marsh, art connoisseur and patron.

Though inevitably bracketed as a 'Georgian', Hodgson mistrusted literary cliques, preferring the company of Fleet Street colleagues and dog-breeding experts. (He was a fine judge of bull-mastiffs and kept them throughout his life).

In 1913, along with the artist Claude Lovat Fraser and the writer Holbrook Jackson, he founded the publishing house The Sign Of The Flying Fame, and produced a series of chapbooks and broadsides featuring his own work as well as pieces by James Stephens and Walter De La Mare. The Fames were extremely influential, being both striking and innovative in their juxtaposition of visual decoration and verse, and brought Hodgson into closer contact with some of the century's greatest writers and poets.

His first literary acquaintance of note was the 'tramp' poet

W.H. Davies, who shared with him a love of strong pipe tobacco and billiards. Edward Thomas, then a reviewer and writer of hack biographies, had introduced the two men at the St George's Tea Rooms, a favourite haunt of his. Around the St George's table Hodgson became acquainted with Walter De La Mare, Gordon Bottomley, John Freeman and Charles Dalmon.

During the First World War Hodgson served with various navy and army anti-aircraft batteries up and down the east coast of England and rose to the rank of lieutenant. He ceased writing poetry altogether during these years and it would not be until the mid-1930s that he commenced work on anything substantial. By then he was guest lecturer in English Literature at the Japanese University of Sendai, having accepted the post in 1923 on condition that the poet Edmund Blunden also accept a similar post in Tokyo. There, Blunden was to write his famous war memoir, *Undertones of War*.

Hodgson remained in Japan until 1938, latterly working on translations of the ancient *Manyoshui* poems for the Japanese Ministry of Education. It was for this that he received the award of the Insignia (5th Class) of the Order of the Rising Sun.

Throughout his years in Japan, Hodgson corresponded with Siegfried Sassoon and acted as confidante and inspiration during the long years when Sassoon was writing his own three-part war autobiography, *The Memoirs of George Sherstone*. During a furlough in Britain, Hodgson travelled north with Sassoon in the latter's car on a book-hunting expedition, an excursion that was intended to provide the pair with material for a joint book of literary extracts. The book did not materialise, but the friendship and correspondence continued until Hodgson's death in the early 1960s.

Perhaps Hodgson's most intriguing friendship, however, was with T.S. Eliot. In early 1932 Hodgson and his third wife Aurelia were introduced to Eliot and his first wife, Vivienne, by literary hostess, Ottoline Morell. Eliot's marriage was collapsing and he spent a great deal of time in Hodgson's company. When

Hodgson left for Japan in August 1932, Eliot wrote him a poem entitled 'Lines to Ralph Hodgson Esquire' – an affectionate little piece modelled on a similar poem by Edward Lear.

Eliot admired Hodgson's poetry and tried in vain to have it published in collected form by his firm, Faber. Eliot also attempted to persuade Hodgson to illustrate his *Old Possum's Book of Practical Cats,* again without success, although he included a dedication in the book to "The Man In White Spats" – Eliot's nickname for Hodgson.

Hodgson remained in Japan until 1938. He then travelled to the USA where he settled on a farm in Ohio with his third wife, Aurelia. Here, he set about producing his final poem, 'The Muse and the Mastiff', which he never finished. Sections of it appeared regularly, in the form of single sheet 'Flying Scrolls' which Hodgson sent to friends all over the world.

These and other pieces were finally collected by Colin Fenton and published under the title *The Skylark and Other Poems* in 1958. His *Collected Poems* appeared to great acclaim in 1961 the year before his death on the 3rd November 1962.

The Poetry

In 1960, when Hodgson reached 90, a score of poets including Eliot, Sassoon, Cecil Day Lewis, Marianne Moore and William Carlos Williams, put together a collection of letters and verse in celebration. Robert Lowell wrote to him:

> You have sung in my ears for twenty-five years or more. First when I read you aloud to myself and others as an undergraduate. Then, when I heard Dylan Thomas read you and finally when I.A. Richards and I spent an evening reading you aloud ... Let me congratulate you on your poems, the ring and shine and humour and lastingness of them ...

Hodgson believed in the beauty of poetry and its power to move and enchant readers. He also possessed a unique imaginative vision of man and history best illustrated in his most praised poem, 'The Song of Honour', a rapturous recital of the world's harmonious 'hymn of being':

> I heard it all, each, every note
> Of every lung and tongue and throat,
> Ay, every rhythm and rhyme
> Of everything that lives and loves
> And upward, ever upward moves
> From lowly to sublime!
> Earth's multitudinous Sons of Light,
> I heard them lift their lyric might
> With each and every chanting sprite
> That lit the sky that wondrous night
> As far as eye could climb!

The poem had a huge influence on a generation of writers that followed him and, although the rise of modernism was to see his work gradually fade in popularity, he was convinced that poetry and poets of whatever school or fashion were part of a seamless tradition. Stephen Spender noted when visiting Hodgson in Ohio in the late 1950s: "I was reminded by the gleam in his eye, the sacred devotion with which he spoke old-fashionedly about the Muse, that he belonged to a kingdom of poetry in which all who were poets were equal ..."

Hodgson drew much of his early inspiration from animal life, particularly birds. He was an expert on the latter and spent many hours as a youth and a man seeking out rare species. They served both as a symbol of nature's enduring mystery as well as a harbinger of joy and hope. The first three poems in the *Selection* – 'The Weaving of the Wing', 'The Linnet', and 'The Sedge-Warbler' – illustrate this fascination.

When Hodgson died in 1962, his wife Aurelia had an extract from 'The Skylark' engraved on his tombstone. Of this quint-essentially English poem, John Masefield wrote, "It will sing with Shelley's and Hardy's in everlasting sunshine."

Hodgson's love of birds led him to protest vigorously at their wanton destruction at the turn of the century for use in the fashion industry. This, in turn, led him to campaign on behalf of all animals in poems such as 'The Last Blackbird' and 'The Hymn To Moloch' among others. 'Stupidity Street' and 'The Bells of Heaven' are short, sharp and polemical, while 'Lines' sums up his approach to animal life in general.

Hodgson's deep sympathy for animals did not exclude compassion for human beings – a sentiment rarely evident in his verse yet eloquently put in the two simple pieces: 'The House Across The Way' and 'To Hang A Man'. His keen appreciation of the opposite sex, however, resulted in three classic poems, 'The Gipsy Girl', 'Eve' and 'Silver Wedding', each one touching upon a particular aspect of the feminine. The last of these was a bittersweet farewell to his first, devoted wife, Janet, who died in 1920 in tragic circumstances.

Despite his anger and compassion, however, there also runs through his verse a decidedly humorous streak: 20 years as a children's cartoonist are evidence of an inherent sense of fun and mischief that, at times, could turn almost surreal. 'The Hever Picnic' is a puzzle, requiring a close knowledge of English history, in general, and of Henry VIII's wives, in particular, while the 'The Ousel Cock' prompted the following response from the American poet, William Carlos Williams:

> We're all alike, we poets, living in a land which is not our own but we especially whom they want to discipline until we are all ready to concede that 'slack' is not really black but some other color of the rainbow. Stick it out even to the edge of doom.

Throughout his life, Hodgson was drawn to reflect upon history and the passing of time. He also enjoyed speculating about human evolution and the rise and fall of civilisations. 'The Hammers' deals succinctly with the latter, while 'Time You Old Gipsy Man', and 'Time', written some 40 years apart, demonstrate that, though his pre-occupations might remain unchanged, his poetic technique would alter quite radically.

His last poem, the 'The Muse and the Mastiff', taking off from a single line of Coleridge's 'Christabel' is, to quote Mick Imla, "as vigorous and strangely charming as it is cranky and incoherent". Critic and writer Naomi Lewis would sum up Hodgson's verse thus:

> It is the shout itself, the idiosyncratic assault that catches and compels. For energy is Mr Hodgson's unfailing quality. In poetry, it can come from a number of sources: loss as well as love; pessimism as much as faith. Mr Hodgson's impetus is usually anger – a thunder of rage on behalf of animals and birds oppressed by men. Oddly untouched by two major wars, this special anger continues, through fifty years, to burn.

The Weaving of the Wing

HER seas and mountains made,
Her skiey labours done,
A new design was hers.
She called a sprite and said
'Go up into the sun
And draw me gossamers.'
He brought a hundred strands,
Sun-yellow, to her hands.

She called her weavers up.
A wild burst into bloom;
Above a flaming whin
She hung a shallow cup,
Her weavers, silk and loom
And law she laid therein,
And turned and kept her way
An aeon and a day.

As down the wild I came,
This day, the crown of Spring,
I tapped a knotted spray
Above a whin aflame,
And saw a ribboned wing,
Sun-yellow, slip away
And hand and eye confessed
A young-forsaken nest.

I let my lips rejoice
I cried 'The work is done',
And praised the weavers' skill.
Thereat I heard a voice:
'The work is but begun,
My weavers labour still,
Not yet the warp and woof
They render question-proof.

Look in the nest again.'
I deeper looked therein,
I saw her silk of sun,
Her loom and weavers plain,
And heard a muffled din
And knew a web begun –
The warp and woof whereof
At last she will approve.

Ay, this I surely know:
An aeon and a day
From this, the crown of Spring,
As down the wild I go
I'll tap that knotted spray
And start a yellow wing!

'The work is done' I'll hear
And let my lips rejoice,
'Is done' I'll echo there
The Universal Voice.

The Linnet

THEY say the world's a sham, and life a lease
    Of nightmare nothing nicknamed Time, and we
Ghost voyagers in undiscovered seas
    Where fact is feign; mirage, reality:

Where all is vain and vanity is all,
    And eyes look out and only know they stare
At conjured coasts whose beacons rise and fall
    And vanish with the hopes that feigned them there:

Where sea-shell measures urge phantom dance
    Till fancied pleasure drowns imagined pain –
Till Death stares madness out of countenance,
    And vanity is all and all is vain.

It may be even as my friends allege.
    I'm pressed to prove that life is something more –
And yet a linnet on a hawthorn hedge
    Still wants explaining and accounting for.

The Sedge-Warbler

IN early summer moonlight I have strayed
Down pass and wildway of the wooded hill
With wonder as again the sedge-bird made

His old, old ballad new beside the mill.
And I have stolen closer to the song
That, lisped low, would swell and change to shrill,

Thick, chattered cheeps that seemed not to belong
Of right to the frail elfin throat that threw
Them on the stream, their waker. There among

The willows I have watched as over flew
A noctule making zigzag round the lone,
Dark elm whose shadow clipt grotesque the new

Green lawn below. On softest breezes blown
From some far brake, the cruising fern-owl's cry
Would stay my steps; a beetle's nearing drone

Would steal upon my sense and pass and die.
There I have heard in that still, solemn hour
The quickened thorn from slaving weeds untie

A prisoned leaf or furlèd bloom, whose dower
Of incense yet burned in the warm June night;
By darkness cozened from his grot to cower

And curve the night long, that shy eremite
The lowly, banded eft would seek his prey;
And thousand worlds my silent world would light
Till broke the babel of the summer day

The Bells of Heaven

'TWOULD ring the bells of Heaven
The wildest peal for years,
If Parson lost his senses
And people came to theirs,
And he and they together
Knelt down with angry prayers
For tamed and shabby tigers
And dancing dogs and bears,
And wretched, blind pit ponies,
And little hunted hares.

Stupidity Street

I SAW with open eyes
Singing birds sweet
Sold in the shops
For the people to eat,
Sold in the shops of
Stupidity Street.

I saw in vision
The worm in the wheat,
And in the shops nothing
For people to eat;
Nothing for sale in
Stupidity Street.

Lines

NO pitted toad behind a stone
        But hoards some secret grace;
The meanest slug with midnight gone
        Has left a silver trace.

No dullest eyes to beauty blind,
        Uplifted to the beast,
But prove some kin with angel kind,
        Though lowliest and least.

The House Across the Way

THE leaves looked in at the window
Of the house across the way,
At a man that had sinned like you and me
And all poor human clay.

He muttered: 'In a gambol
I took my soul astray,
But to-morrow I'll drag it back from danger,
In the morning, come what may;
For no man knows what season
He shall go his ghostly way.'
And his face fell down upon the table,
And where it fell it lay.

And the wind blew under the carpet
And it said, or it seemed to say:
'Truly, all men must go a-ghosting
And no man knows his day.'
And the leaves stared in at the window
Like the people at a play.

The Last Blackbird

MY head was tired; I had no mind to think
    Of Beauty wronged and none to give redress:
I got me to a place where linnets drink
    And lizards go in ferny loveliness.

A blackbird sang, so down I fell; meseemed,
    Soothed by his note, I closed a drowsy lid;
And I was ventured on a dream – I dreamed
    One stood and questioned me how linnets did.

And straight I knew who thus in angel guise
    Would have my news – some trick of lip or brow
Guessed me her rank; I said not otherwise
    Than ill indeed it went with linnets now.

And with the words I got upon my feet;
    Her look said she would hear if I had more:
I led her to an ancient mossy seat,
    And blest the hour for my inquisitor.

'Nature,' I said, 'O thou whose hand controlled
    And ordered chaos to a reasoned plan
With "Know thou me, Old Night, and loose thy hold!"
    And in whose accent Life and Love began:

'Whose "Keep thou this, and thou that circuit go,"
    Or "Here stand thou, and thou in that place stand,"
Lifted a meek or laid a hot star low,
    Chartered a sun or cancelled his command:

'Who flattered with an object aimless spheres,
    And gave to each place, precedence and class,
Time and degree, till constancy was theirs,
    And perfect system where no system was:

'Hear me! The blackbird piping from the hill,
　　His insolent wild eye – its yellow rim –
His coaly vest and yellow mandible –
　　Is he not thine? Wouldst thou continue him?

'Art thou still minded, Nature, to provide
　　The salts and sweets a frolic wagtail picks
Out of the spume that quilts an idle tide
　　Behind the trough where meeting waters mix?

'Hast thou a mind to keep a redstart dressed
　　As now and heretofore; to order still
Thy system of economy unguessed
　　That gives a shiver to his flaring quill?

'Wouldst thou still keep the chill-chaff to his song,
　　And have him know to braid his grassy dome?
Wouldst knot and twist with many a weedy thong
　　The green confusion leaping round his home?

'Is still thy mind for wrens and little springs
　　And ferns and sudden stoats and popping mice,
And all the myriad noisy rainbow wings
　　That make the wood not less than Paradise?

'Wouldst in thy season strip the little wood
　　And hap it over with a frozen coat,
To spot a corner there with icy blood,
　　And stretch a rabbit with a frozen stoat?

'Hear me,' I said. 'Thy wood's a grandam's tale;
　　Its trees are felled; save one its birds are dead;
Thou art unqueened; now other hands prevail;
　　One blackbird lives – he is the last,' I said.

And she, 'The poisèd moths thy hand caressed,
    Sip they not wines from fuchsias by the sea?
Runs clear no stream to bright a linnet's breast
    Or sparkle in the moon? Nay, gladden me!

'Sure Beauty's in the pine the heron crost,
    Or Beauty's on the heath or down or plain,
Or Beauty's on the yellow desert lost
    In desert glare? Nay, make me glad again.'

I said the place was changed where hawk-moths sipped
    Eve's sugared cup; nor now was Beauty's mark
Upon the stream where once her linnets dipped,
    And moony bubbles raced into the dark;

'Wild Beauty's left the down whereon she lay;
    The heaths and plains are bare; shy Beauty's fled
The woods; fierce Beauty's left her desert day;
    Beauty is fled or dead. Beauty is dead.

'Yon blackbird with to-night will end his race.'
    I stopped, and Nature rose and looked abroad:
She came again and asked who ruled the place;
    I named then him who reigned its overlord.

'Thou madest all things equal under thee;
    To all thy gifts were Beauty, Love, and Youth.'
'I pricked a vein that I might gladden me
    With flower of that my seed thou callest Truth.'

'Thou chosest one not fairer than his kin
    To keep the story of thine eyes' delight.'
'I gave a book to choice of mine wherein
    To chronicle that pleasing in my sight.'

'Who learned the letters equal to his task
    To open ways beyond his right employ,
Who got him to a fiction and a mask
    And hid the book he did not dare destroy!

'Not then he heard the noises in the cloud,
    Nor cried his wonder when the leaf uncurled
After the wind, nor went he wonder-browed
    Adoring when the rainbow spanned the world.'

She said, 'I gave him ears – ' 'He waxed them in.'
    'And sight: I taught him beauty was my sum.'
'New gods he found: they taught him sight was sin.'
    'And speech and song.' 'He blasphemed or was dumb.

'On every wind his evil fame was blown;
    His every step struck fear and panic doubt;
Suspect and shunned, he armed and went alone,
    Or with sly wisdom walled himself about.

'He woodman turned and wide he laid his axe;
    Stream, hill, and heath, to all he put his hand,
Taxed pitilessly all; all paid the tax;
    Only the sea ignored his ill demand.

'He saw thy hills and brought a newer plan;
    Hill, stream, and heath he tricked to evil whim;
Only the sea ignored or countered Man,
    Only the sea despised and countered him.

'And soon for sport a hunting he would go;
    The chase is over save for yon last bird
Whose wing to-morrow – Shout me this last woe!' –
    I shrank beneath the angers I had stirred –

'Whose wing to-morrow – shout! This final prize – '
　　'Will deck his stony mate for holiday.'
Ten thousand hells roared out of Nature's eyes,
　　She pressed her lids and shut the rage away.

'But knows he never midnight questioning?
　　Is every sense I gave him dead or dark?'
I said, 'He knows he reigns to-day a king,
　　And has forgot the day he was thy clerk.'

'Henceforward is this world his gaud, his toy;
　　If bones he wills, in bones the world will lie;
His to deflower, infect, defile, destroy –
　　Unless – ' she said, 'Thou hast a remedy?'

I said, 'Save one, not I: reject, annul
　　Him, seed and breed and story, or have done
And send this world, thy Bubble Beautiful,
　　With sudden moth-want whirling at its sun.'

She answered me, 'The last was spoken ill.
　　My world is good; its streams may yet run pure;
My blackbird now is piping from the hill!'
　　She listened to his lazy overture.

Miraculous old song! Our wonder met:
　　She turned away and listened to the bird.
'To-night.' I said, 'to-night he'll pay the debt.'
　　'To-night,' I said, but him alone she heard.

'Only the sea!' Then Nature, rising, stood:
　　'The chase is over; yon last bird is free.
Before I give new beauty to the wood,
　　How say'st thou, poet, to a wider sea?'

She looked above: small as a pigeon's wing
    A cloud came up and crost the blackbird's tree.
She said, 'How say'st thou if yon blackbird bring,
    To wash my world, a deeper, wider sea?'

I woke. A dizzy man I reeling went
    Round by the hill: a blackbird hurried by;
Clouds raced and cracked; to some high argument
    Were hurrying the gossips of the sky.

To Hang a Man

TO hang a man:
To fit the cap,
And fix the rope,
And slide the bar,
And let him drop.
I know, I know:
What can you do!
You have no choice,
You're driven to;
You can't be soft –
A man like that;
But Oh it seems –
I don't know what –
To hang a man!

The Hever Picnic

SHOCK howled: the merry buzz stopped dead:
All but Anne went terrified,
As round the bush at a tall man's stride
      Came Luckie Lee,
         Queen of the Egyptians.

Anne, cutting her a slice of pound-cake, said:
'Why d'you stare so – what d'you see!
'Staring like a hawk at me,
'Good woman?'
         'H'm', their guest replied,
'Weddings… beddings… and…'
           'And what?'
The lovely Bullen begged.
           'And that
'Is all, as far as I can see',
And – muttering to herself aside:
'Not for both her silver bracelets' –
Round the bush at twice the stride
      Went Luckie Lee,
         Queen of the Egyptians.

'The Ousel Cock' –

I ASKED a cock blackbird,
'Why did you choose black?
' – In the ages of old
'When blackbirds were new
'And questions of hue
'Began to unfold –
'With the rainbow to choose from,
'Why did you pick black?'

'You mean', he replied,
'That a blackbird's no posy …
'But that point aside;
'This charge that we slighted
'The rainbow of old:
'Are you nearsighted?
' – 'Black goes with gold
'In a manner that dizzies
'Our hens to behold
'In the Spring of the year;
'That's why we chose black
'In the ages far back,
'And how we got here,
'If you need to be told.'

The Birdcatcher

WHEN flighting time is on I go
With clap-net and decoy,
A-fowling after goldfinches
And other birds of joy;

I lurk among the thickets of
The Heart where they are bred,
And catch the twittering beauties as
They fly into my Head.

The Gipsy Girl

'COME, try your skill, kind gentlemen,
A penny for three tries!'
Some threw and lost, some threw and won
A ten-a-penny prize.

She was a tawny gipsy girl,
A girl of twenty years,
I liked her for the lumps of gold
That jingled from her ears;

I liked the flaring yellow scarf.
Bound loose about her throat,
I liked her showy purple gown
And flashy velvet coat.

A man came up, too loose of tongue,
And said no good to her;
She did not blush as Saxons do,
Or turn upon the cur;

She fawned and whined 'Sweet gentleman,
A penny for three tries!'
– But oh, the den of wild things in
The darkness of her eyes!

Eve

EVE, with her basket, was
Deep in the bells and grass,
Wading in bells and grass
Up to her knees,
Picking a dish of sweet
Berries and plums to eat,
Down in the bells and grass
Under the trees.

Mute as a mouse in a
Corner the cobra lay,
Curled round a bough of the
Cinnamon tall...
Now to get even and
Humble proud Heaven and
Now was the moment or
Never at all.

'Eva!' Each syllable
Light as a flower fell,
'Eva!' he whispered the
Wondering maid,
Soft as a bubble sung
Out of a linnet's lung,
Soft and most silverly
'Eva!' he said.

Picture that orchard sprite,
Eve, with her body white,
Supple and smooth to her
Slim finger tips,
Wondering, listening,
Listening, wondering,
Eve with a berry
Half-way to her lips.

Oh had our simple Eve
Seen through the make-believe!
Had she but known the
Pretender he was!
Out of the boughs he came,
Whispering still her name,
Tumbling in twenty rings
Into the grass.

Here was the strangest pair
In the world anywhere,
Eve in the bells and grass
Kneeling, and he
Telling his story low...
Singing birds saw them go
Down the dark path to
The Blasphemous Tree.

Oh what a clatter when
Titmouse and Jenny Wren
Saw him successful and
Taking his leave!
How the birds rated him,
How they all hated him!
How they all pitied
Poor motherless Eve!

Picture her crying
Outside in the lane,
Eve, with no dish of sweet
Berries and plums to eat,
Haunting the gate of the
Orchard in vain...
Picture the lewd delight
Under the hill to-night –
'Eva!' the toast goes round,
'Eva!' again.

Silver Wedding

IN the middle of the night
He started up
At a cry from his sleeping Bride –
A bat from some ruin
In a heart he'd never searched,
Nay, hardly seen inside:

'Want me and take me
For the woman that I am
And not for her that died,
The lovely chit nineteen
I one time was,
And am no more' – she cried.

Time, you Old Gipsy Man

TIME, you old gipsy man,
   Will you not stay,
Put up your caravan
   Just for one day?

All things I'll give you
Will you be my guest,
Bells for your jennet
Of silver the best,
Goldsmiths shall beat you
A great golden ring,
Peacocks shall bow to you,
Little boys sing,
Oh, and sweet girls will
Festoon you with may,
Time, you old gipsy,
Why hasten away?

Last week in Babylon,
Last night in Rome,
Morning, and in the crush
Under Paul's dome;
Under Paul's dial
You tighten your rein –
Only a moment,
And off once again;
Off to some city
Now blind in the womb,
Off to another
Ere that's in the tomb.

Time, you old gipsy man,
   Will you not stay,
Put up your caravan
   Just for one day?

Time

SPIRALWISE it spins
And twirls about the Sun,
Both with and withershins
At once, a dual run
Anomalously one;
Its speed is such it gains
Upon itself: outsped,
Outdistanced, it remains
At every point ahead,
No less at all points led,
At none with either strains
Or lapses in the rush
Of its almighty vanes
To mar the poise or hush;
Comparing it for speed:
Lightning is a snail
That pauses on its trail
From bank to underbrush,
Mindful of its need,
With dawn astir, to feed
Before the morning thrush;
Comparing it for poise:
The tops we spun to sleep,
Seemingly so deep
Stockstill, when we were boys,
No more than stumbled round,
Boxwoods though they were,
The best we ever wound
Or whipped of all such toys;
Comparing it for sound:
The wisp of gossamer
Caught in a squirrel's fur,
Groans like a ship aground;
Shadow makes more noise.

The Hammers

NOISE of hammers once I heard,
Many hammers, busy hammers,
Beating, shaping, night and day,
Shaping, beating dust and clay
To a palace; saw it reared;
Saw the hammers laid away.

And I listened, and I heard
Hammers beating, night and day,
In the palace newly reared,
Beating it to dust and clay:
Other hammers, muffled hammers,
Silent hammers of decay.

After

'How fared you when you mortal were?
    What did you see on my peopled star?'
'Oh well enough,' I answered her,
    'It went for me where mortals are!

'I saw blue flowers and the merlin's flight
    And the rime on the wintry tree,
Blue doves I saw and summer light
    On the wings of the cinnamon bee.'

The Mystery

HE came and took me by the hand
    Up to a red rose tree,
He kept His meaning to Himself
    But gave a rose to me.

I did not pray Him to lay bare
    The mystery to me,
Enough the rose was Heaven to smell,
    And His own face to see.

The Skylark

THE world of old that stopped and stared,
With simple wits revolving
The singer and the song, declared
The riddle past resolving.

A later skylark takes the sky,
A wiser world lies under;
And still we put our wisdom by
And give the bird our wonder.

But, ah! within our inmost ear
Some pit of sense is ringing
With new surmise that more we hear
Than mortal skylark singing, –

That muffled in his shrill amours
Another voice is speaking,
That access there is surely ours,
Ours surely for the seeking.

Our dusts are one; we dare to think
Us destined to one glory;
For more: by faith alone we link
Two chapters of one story.

His but to be and sing and soar –
So but the skies invite him –
As he all day and evermore
Would in his lung delight him;

To own before his sovran sun
No lowly tie or tether
Beyond the fair that dotes upon
His crest of pointed feather;

To leap anew and lost within
The beams and blue abysses
Enchant her with redoubled din
Of benisons and blisses,

And flutter fainting from the sky –
His frenzy past and over –
Into her poppied bowery
Or shock of ruddy clover,

And make her bridal bed between
The boles of pipy grasses
Or in a maze of scented green
And secret ports and passes;

To pay the world nor tax nor toll
Save with his melic labours,
To claim in turn nor due nor dole
Save peace and gentle neighbours;

To hoard no boon beyond his wing,
No bauble but his beauty,
His but to be and soar and sing
And wave his dear his duty,

And shout him blest and over-blest
Until the skies reject him,
And hear the while within his breast
No privy woe correct him;

To ken no thorn offending there,
No new, no ancient fester
With stubborn smart his years despair
To soften or sequester,

No burnings for a bygone day,
No bodings of hereafter,
No wounds like them we hide away
Beneath our smiles and laughter.

Sun-climber he, his ladders run
Through spaces ever sparkling!
We make no song and climb no sun
But ways within us darkling;

How dark we know, how utter dark,
When blundering heels beside us
Crush out some timely watchet spark
Of glow-worm dropt to guide us;

Or when some fenny match ablaze
One sudden moment sighted
As sudden leaves our dazzled gaze
And us the worse benighted.

Yet are we blest: we know we climb
From darker ways behind us,
That suns will break for us in time
Too early broke would blind us,

And lit within we'll stand among
The corn at last receiving
The secret of our skylark's song,
And more we go believing.

The Song of Honour

I CLIMBED a hill as light fell short,
And rooks came home in scramble sort,
And filled the trees and flapped and fought
And sang themselves to sleep;
An owl from nowhere with no sound
Swung by and soon was nowhere found,
I heard him calling half-way round,
Holloing loud and deep;
A pair of stars, faint pins of light,
Then many a star, sailed into sight,
And all the stars, the flower of night,
Were round me at a leap;
To tell how still the valleys lay
I heard a watchdog miles away,
And bells of distant sheep.

I heard no more of bird or bell,
The mastiff in a slumber fell,
I stared into the sky,
As wondering men have always done
Since beauty and the stars were one,
Though none so hard as I.

It seemed, so still the valleys were,
As if the whole world knelt at prayer,
Save me and me alone;
So pure and wide that silence was
I feared to bend a blade of grass,
And there I stood like stone.

There, sharp and sudden, there I heard –
Ah! Some wild lovesick singing bird
Woke singing in the trees?
The nightingale and babble-wren
Were in the English greenwood then,
And you heard one of these?

The babble-wren and the nightingale
Sang in the Abyssinian vale
That season of the year!
Yet, true enough, I heard them plain,
I heard them both again, again,
As sharp and sweet and clear
As if the Abyssinian tree
Had thrust a bough across the sea,
Had thrust a bough across to me
With music for my ear!

I heard them both, and oh! I heard
The song of every singing bird
That sings beneath the sky,
And with the song of lark and wren
The song of mountains, moths and men
And seas and rainbows vie!

I heard the universal choir
The Sons of Light exalt their Sire
With universal song,
Earth's lowliest and loudest notes,
Her million times ten million throats
Exalt Him loud and long,
And lips and lungs and tongues of Grace
From every part and every place
Within the shining of His face,
The universal throng.

I heard the hymn of being sound
From every well of honour found
In human sense and soul:
The song of poets when they write
The testament of Beautysprite
Upon a flying scroll,
The song of painters when they take

A burning brush for Beauty's sake
And limn her features whole –

The song of men divinely wise
Who look and see in starry skies
Not stars so much as robins' eyes,
And when these pale away
Her flocks of shiny pleiades
Among the plums and apple trees
Sing in the summer day –

The song of all both high and low
To some blest vision true,
The song of beggars when they throw
The crust of pity all men owe
To hungry sparrows in the snow,
Old beggars hungry too –
The song of kings of kingdoms when
They rise above their fortune men,
And crown themselves anew –

The song of courage, heart and will
And gladness in a fight,
Of men who face a hopeless hill
With sparking and delight,
The bells and bells of song that ring
Round banners of a cause or king
From armies bleeding white –
The song of sailors every one
When monstrous tide and tempest run
At ships like bulls at red,
When stately ships are twirled and spun
Like whipping tops and help there's none
And mighty ships ten thousand ton
Go down like lumps of lead –

And song of fighters stern as they
At odds with fortune night and day,
Crammed up in cities grim and grey
As thick as bees in hives,
Hosannas of a lowly throng
Who sing unconscious of their song,
Whose lips are in their lives –

And song of some at holy war
With spells and ghouls more dread by far
Than deadly seas and cities are,
Or hordes of quarelling kings –
The song of fighters great and small,
The song of pretty fighters all,
And high heroic things –

The song of lovers – who knows how
Twitched up from place and time
Upon a sigh, a blush, a vow,
A curve or hue of cheek or brow,
Borne up and off from here and now
Into the void sublime!

And crying loves and passions still
In every key from soft to shrill
And numbers never done,
Dog-loyalties to faith and friend,
And loves like Ruth's of old no end,
And intermission none –

And burst on burst for beauty and
For numbers not behind,
From men whose love of motherland
Is like a dog's for one dear hand,
Sole, selfless, boundless, blind –

And song of some with hearts beside
For men and sorrows far and wide,
Who watch the world with pity and pride
And warm to all mankind –

And endless joyous music rise
From children at their play,
And endless soaring lullabies
From happy, happy mothers' eyes,
And answering crows and baby cries,
How many who shall say!
And many a song as wondrous well
With pangs and sweets intolerable
From lonely hearths too gray to tell,
God knows how utter gray!
And song from many a house of care
When pain has forced a footing there
And there's a Darkness on the stair
Will not be turned away –

And song – the song whose singers come
With old kind tales of pity from
The Great Compassion's lips,
That makes the bells of Heaven to peal
Round pillows frosty with the feel
Of Death's cold finger tips –

The song of men all sorts and kinds,
As many tempers, moods and minds
As leaves are on a tree,
As many faiths and castes and creeds,
As many human bloods and breeds
As in the world may be;

The song of each and all who gaze
On Beauty in her naked blaze,
Or see her dimly in a haze,
Or get her light in fitful rays
And tiniest needles even,
The song of all not wholly dark,
Not wholly sunk in stupor stark
Too deep for groping Heaven –

The alleluias sweet and clear
And wild with beauty men mishear,
From choirs of song as near and dear
To Paradise as they,
The everlasting pipe and flute
Of wind and sea and bird and brute,
And lips deaf men imagine mute
In wood and stone and clay:

The music of a lion strong
That shakes a hill a whole night long,
A hill as loud as he,
The twitter of a mouse among
Melodious greenery,
The ruby's and the rainbow's song,
The nightingale's – all three,
The song of life that wells and flows
From every leopard, lark and rose
And everything that gleams or goes
Lack-lustre in the sea.

I heard it all, each, every note
Of every lung and tongue and throat,
Ay, every rhythm and rhyme

Of everything that lives and loves
And upward, ever upward moves
Form lowly to sublime!
Earth's multitudinous Sons of Light,
I heard them lift their lyric might
With each and every chanting sprite
That lit the sky that wondrous night
As far as eye could climb!

I heard it all, I heard the whole
Harmonious hymn of being roll
Up through the chapel of my soul
And at the altar die,
And in the awful quiet then
Myself I heard, Amen, Amen,
Amen I heard me cry!
I heard it all, and then although
I caught my flying sense, Oh,
A dizzy man was I!
I stood and stared; the sky was lit,
The sky was stars all over it,
I stood, I knew not why,
Without a wish, without a will,
I stood upon that silent hill
And stared into the sky until
My eyes were blind with stars and still
I stared into the sky.

The Bull

SEE an old unhappy bull,
Sick in soul and body both,
Slouching in the undergrowth
Of the forest beautiful,
Banished from the herd he led,
Bulls and cows a thousand head.

Cranes and gaudy parrots go
Up and down the burning sky;
Tree-top cats purr drowsily
In the dim-day green below;
And troops of monkeys, nutting, some,
All disputing, go and come;

And things abominable sit
Picking offal buck or swine,
On the mess and over it
Burnished flies and beetles shine,
And spiders big as bladders lie
Under hemlocks ten foot high;

And a dotted serpent curled
Round and round and round a tree,
Yellowing its greenery,
Keeps a watch on all the world,
All the world and this old bull
In the forest beautiful.

Bravely by his fall he came:
One he led, a bull of blood
Newly come to lustihood,
Fought and put his prince to shame,
Snuffed and pawed the prostrate head
Tameless even while it bled.

There they left him, every one,
Left him there without a lick,
Left him for the birds to pick,
Left him there for carrion,
Vilely from their bosom cast
Wisdom, worth and love at last.

When the lion left his lair
And roared his beauty through the hills,
And the vultures pecked their quills
And flew into the middle air,
Then this prince no more to reign
Came to life and lived again.

He snuffed the herd in far retreat,
He saw the blood upon the ground,
And snuffed the burning airs around
Still with beevish odours sweet,
While the blood ran down his head
And his mouth ran slaver red.

Pity him, this fallen chief,
All his splendour, all his strength,
All his body' breadth and length
Dwindled down with shame and grief,
Half the bull he was before,
Bones and leather, nothing more.

See him standing dewlap-deep
In the rushes at the lake,
Surly, stupid, half asleep,
Waiting for his heart to break
And the birds to join the flies
Feasting at his bloodshot eyes, –

Standing with his head hung down
In a stupor dreaming things:
Green savannas, jungles brown,
Battlefields and bellowings,
Bulls undone and lions dead
And vultures flapping overhead.

Dreaming things: of days he spent
With his mother gaunt and lean
In the valley warm and green,
Full of baby wonderment,
Blinking out of silly eyes
At a hundred mysteries;

Dreaming over once again
How he wandered with a throng
Of bulls and cows a thousand strong,
Wandered on from plain to plain,
Up the hill and down the dale,
Always at his mother's tail;

How he lagged behind the herd,
Lagged and tottered, weak of limb,
And she turned and ran to him
Blaring at the loathly bird
Stationed always in t skies,
Waiting for the flesh that dies.

Dreaming maybe of a day
When her drained and drying paps
Turned him to the sweets and saps,
Richer fountains by the way,
And she left the bull she bore
And he looked on her no more;

And his little frame grew stout,
And his little legs grew strong,
And the way was not so long;
And his little horns came out,
And he played at butting trees
And boulder-stones and tortoises,

Joined a game of knobby skulls
With the youngsters of his year,
All the other little bulls,
Learning both to bruise and bear,
Learning how to stand a shock
Like a little bull of rock.

Dreaming of a day less dim,
Dreaming of a time less far,
When the faint but certain star
Of destiny burned clear for him,
And a fierce and wild unrest
Broke the quiet of his breast,

And the gristles of his youth
Hardened in his comely pow,
And he came to fighting growth,
Beat his bull and won his cow,
And flew his tail and trampled off
Past the tallest, vain enough,

And curved about in splendour full
And curved again and snuffed the airs
As who should say Come out who dares!
And all beheld a bull, a Bull,
And knew that here was surely one
That backed for no bull, fearing none.

And the leader of the herd
Looked and saw, and beat the ground,
And shook the forest with his sound,
Bellowed at the loathly bird
Stationed always in the skies,
Waiting for the flesh that dies.

Dreaming, this old bull forlorn,
Surely dreaming of the hour
When he came to sultan power,
And they owned him master-horn,
Chiefest bull of all among
Bulls and cows a thousand strong.

And in all the tramping herd
Not a bull that barred his way,
Not a cow that said him nay,
Not a bull or cow that erred
In the furnace of his look
Dared a second, worse rebuke;

Not in all the forest wide,
Jungle, thicket, pasture, fen,
Not another dared him then,
Dared him and again defied;
Not a sovereign buck or boar
Came a second time for more.

Not a serpent that survived
Once the terrors of his hoof
Risked a second time reproof,
Came a second time and lived,
Not serpent in its skin
Came again for discipline;

Not a leopard bright as flame,
Flashing fingerhooks of steel,
That a wooden tree might feel,
Met his fury once and came
For second reprimand,
Not a leopard in the land.

Not a lion of them all,
Not a lion of the hills,
Hero of a thousand kills,
Dared a second fight and fall,
Dared that ram terrific twice,
Paid a second time the price ...

Pity him, this dupe of dream,
Leader of the herd again
Only in his daft old brain,
Once again the bull supreme
And bull enough to bear the part
Only in his tameless heart.

Pity him that he must wake;
Even now the swarm of flies
Blackening his bloodshot eyes
Bursts and blusters round the lake,
Scattered from the feast half-fed,
By great shadows overhead.

And the dreamer turns away
From his visionary herds
And his splendid yesterday,
Turns to meet the loathly birds
Flocking round him from the skies,
Waiting for the flesh that dies.

Reason has Moons

REASON has moons, but moons not hers
   Lie mirror'd on her sea,
Confounding her astronomers,
   But, O! delighting me.

*   *   *

BABYLON – where I go dreaming
When I weary of today,
Weary of a world grown gray.

*   *   *

GOD loves an idle rainbow
No less than labouring seas.

A Wood Song

NOW one and all, you Roses,
   Wake up, you lie too long!
This very morning closes
   The Nightingale his song;

Each from its olive chamber
   His babies every one
This very morning clamber
   Into the shining sun.

You Slug-a-beds and Simples,
   Why will you so delay!
Dears, doff your olive wimples,
   And listen while you may.

The Hymn to Moloch

O THOU who didst furnish
The fowls of the air
With loverly feathers
For leydies to wear,
Receive this Petition
For blessin an aid,
From the principal Ouses
Engaged in the Trade.

The trouble's as follows:
A white-livered Scum,
What if they was choked
'Twould be better for some,
S'been pokin about an
Creatin a fuss
An talkin too loud to be
Ealthy for us.

Thou'lt ardly believe
Ow damn friendly they are,
They say there's a time
In the future not far
When birds worth good money'll
Waste by the ton
An the Trade can look
Perishin pleased to look on,

With best lines in Paradies
Equal to what
Is fetchin a pony
A time in the at,

An ospreys an ummins
An other choice goods
Wastefully oppin
About in the woods.

They're kiddin the papers,
An callin us names,
Not Yorkshire ones neither,
That's one of their games,
They've others as pleasin
An soakin with spite,
An it don't make us appy,
Ow can it do, quite!

We thank thee most earty
For mercies to date,
The Olesales is pickin
Nice profits per crate,
Reports from the Retails
Is pleasin to read;
We certainly thank thee
Most earty indeed.

Vouchsafe, then, to muzzle
These meddlesome swine,
An learn em to andle goods
More in their line,
Be faithful, be foxy
Till peril is past,
An plant thy strong sword
In their livers at last.

The Muse and the Mastiff

'For what can ail the mastiff bitch?'

J., living in the country, some distance from London, owns a mastiff bitch puppy five or six months old: latterly she has become subject to violent dreams at night, in the stable yard.

J., a bit puzzled, sends his friend R., a poet living in an attic in Chelsea, a postcard describing these dreams: his wife, a wider reader than he, adds the inevitable postscript.

R. at once interprets the dream by the theory of inherited experience, and the appearance of the Muse is instantaneous. This is the outline of an introductory portion of the poem, here omitted. The poem is presented as being read by R. to J. on a visit to the country, six weeks later.

SOMETHING of him still comes out
Of his moorland fog – some hazy, dim,
Old family death's-head print of him
In her blood and bones – and into sight,
Hoisting itself across the wall
And shuffling a hairy foot about
The shrubbery and paths at night,
In her sleep: Here, Now: a call
Precisely such as once upon a time
When he was in his fleshly prime
And she in hers – as still she is –
He paid upon the moorland villages,
Himself, the lost Original,
In certain of his moods, not all.
Not, for example, as he came
With a backward Easter, sulky, sour,
But shy of parish note and fame
And homesick almost from the hour;
His purpose – quiet meals and cheap –
How ever frail and insecure
On soil so rich in cattle and sheep,
Sustained by second thoughts ten deep

At every step: the first rebuff,
Or disappointment, up and off –
On to the village rubbish heap;
Not the pad to stand on pride
And suffer for a clocking hen,
Or stumble into mastiff ken,
Company less, and less again
Likely to enter that full stride –
Least of all round village doors
So distant from his mountain den –
And come, unless he played a part
That cut the road off at the start,
Buffeting his way through time and tide
A thousand years to threaten yours,
And mystify the best of men
And rush the Muse – in all her glow
And innocence of Ah, how long ago! –
Winged on one imperishable line
Of *Christabel* post-haste to mine,
Not for him that glory, then.

Epilogue

WELL we know that they made him pay,
Then – or in his other shoes –
Dunned him till they got their dues,
Thus hastening his breed's decay
And fall into the winter sleep
That asks no tallow for winter keep:
Where only one mouth melts for prey
And clocks all stop or run to lose,
Never but a little while
Ticking to the tiny frets
Of Nature's last and smallest file:
But whether that night he stole away
Red with glory home again,
Leaving behind a load of debts
And bony dreams, or there and then
Paid his owings, who's to say?
Even your mastiff now forgets
Or only your mastiff knows to-day.

Ralph Hodgson and T.S. Eliot

GREENWICH EXCHANGE BOOKS

Paperback unless otherwise stated.

POETRY

Adam's Thoughts in Winter *by Warren Hope*

Warren Hope's poems have appeared from time to time in a number of literary periodicals, pamphlets and anthologies on both sides of the Atlantic. They appeal to lovers of poetry everywhere. His poems are brief, clear, frequently lyrical, characterised by wit, but often distinguished by tenderness. The poems gathered in this first book-length collection counter the brutalising ethos of contemporary life, speaking of and for the virtues of modesty, honesty and gentleness in an individual, memorable way.
2000 • 47 pages • ISBN 1-871551-40-4

Baudelaire: Les Fleurs du Mal *Translated by F.W. Leakey*

Selected poems from *Les Fleurs du Mal* are translated with parallel French texts and are designed to be read with pleasure by readers who have no French as well as those who are practised in the French language.
F.W. Leakey was Professor of French in the University of London. As a scholar, critic and teacher he specialised in the work of Baudelaire for 50 years and published a number of books on the poet.
2001 • 153 pages • ISBN 1-871551-10-2

'The Last Blackbird' and other poems by Ralph Hodgson *edited and introduced by John Harding*

Ralph Hodgson (1871-1962) was a poet and illustrator whose most influentialand enduring work appeared to great acclaim just prior to and during the First World War. His work is imbued with a spiritual passion for the beauty of creation and the mystery of existence. This new selection brings together, for the first time in 40 years, some of the most beautiful and powerful 'hymns to life' in the English language.
John Harding lives in London. He is a freelance writer and teacher and is Ralph Hodgson's biographer.
2004 • 70 pages • ISBN 1-871551-81-1

Lines from the Stone Age *by Sean Haldane*

Reviewing Sean Haldane's 1992 volume *Desire in Belfast*, Robert Nye wrote in *The Times* that "Haldane can be sure of his place among the English poets." This place is not yet a conspicuous one, mainly because his early volumes appeared in Canada and because he has earned his living by other means than literature. Despite this, his poems have always had their circle of readers. The 60 previously unpublished poems of *Lines from the Stone Age* – "lines of longing, terror, pride, lust and pain" – may widen this circle.

2000 • 53 pages • ISBN 1-871551-39-0

Shakespeare's Sonnets *by Martin Seymour-Smith*
Martin Seymour-Smith's outstanding achievement lies in the field of literary biography and criticism. In 1963 he produced his comprehensive edition, in the old spelling, of *Shakespeare's Sonnets* (here revised and corrected by himself and Peter Davies in 1998). With its landmark introduction and its brilliant critical commentary on each sonnet, it was praised by William Empson and John Dover Wilson. Stephen Spender said of him "I greatly admire Martin Seymour-Smith for the independence of his views and the great interest of his mind"; and both Robert Graves and Anthony Burgess described him as the leading critic of his time. His exegesis of the *Sonnets* remains unsurpassed.

2001 • 194 pages • ISBN 1-871551-38-2

Wilderness *by Martin Seymour-Smith*
This is Martin Seymour-Smith's first publication of his poetry for more than twenty years. This collection of 36 poems is a fearless account of an inner life of love, frustration, guilt, laughter and the celebration of others. He is best known to the general public as the author of the controversial and bestselling *Hardy* (1994).

1994 • 52 pages • ISBN 1-871551-08-0

STUDENT GUIDES

Greenwich Exchange Student Guides are critical studies of major or contemporary serious writers in English and selected European languages. The series is for the student, the teacher and 'common readers' and is an ideal resource for libraries. The *Times Educational Supplement* praised these books, saying, "The style of these guides has a pressure of meaning behind it. Students should learn from that ... If art is about selection, perception and taste, then this is it."

(ISBN prefix 1-871551- applies)
The series includes:
W.H. Auden by Stephen Wade (36-6)
Honoré de Balzac by Wendy Mercer (48-X)
William Blake by Peter Davies (27-7)

LITERATURE & BIOGRAPHY

Aleister Crowley and the Cult of Pan *by Paul Newman*
Few more nightmarish figures stalk English literature than Aleister Crowley (1875-1947), poet, magician, mountaineer and agent provocateur. In this groundbreaking study, Paul Newman dives into the occult mire of Crowley's works and fishes out gems and grotesqueries that are by turns ethereal, sublime, pornographic and horrifying. An influential exponent of the cult of the Great God Pan, his essentially 'pagan' outlook was shared by major European writers as well as English novelists like E.M. Forster, D.H. Lawrence and Arthur Machen.
Paul Newman lives in Cornwall. Editor of the literary magazine *Abraxas*, he has written over ten books.
2004 • 223 pages • ISBN 1-871551-66-8

The Author, the Book and the Reader *by Robert Giddings*
This collection of essays analyses the effects of changing technology and the attendant commercial pressures on literary styles and subject matter. Authors covered include Charles Dickens, Tobias George Smollett, Mark Twain, Dr Johnson and John le Carré.
1991 • 220 pages • illustrated • ISBN 1-871551-01-3

John Dryden *by Anthony Fowles*
Of all the poets of the Augustan age, John Dryden was the most worldly. Anthony Fowles traces Dryden's evolution from 'wordsmith' to major poet.
This critical study shows a poet of vigour and technical panache whose art was forged in the heat and battle of a turbulent polemical and pamphleteering age. Although Dryden's status as a literary critic has long been established, Fowles draws attention to Dryden's neglected achievements as a translator of poetry. He deals also with the less well-known aspects of Dryden's work – his plays and occasional pieces.
Anthony Fowles was born in London and educated at the Universities of Oxford and Southern California. He began his career in filmmaking before becoming an author of film and television scripts and more than twenty books.
2003 • 292 pages • ISBN 1-871551-58-7

The Good That We Do *by John Lucas*
John Lucas' book blends fiction, biography and social history in order to tell the story of his grandfather, Horace Kelly. Headteacher of a succession of elementary schools in impoverished areas of London, 'Hod' Kelly was also a keen cricketer, a devotee of the music hall, and included among his friends the great Trade Union leader, Ernest Bevin. In telling the story of his life, Lucas has provided a fascinating range of insights into the lives of ordinary Londoners from the First World War until the outbreak of the Second World War. Threaded throughout is an account of such people's hunger for education, and of the different ways government, church and educational officialdom ministered to that hunger. *The Good That We Do* is both a study of one man and of a period when England changed, drastically and forever.
John Lucas is Professor of English at Nottingham Trent University and is a poet and critic.
2001 • 214 pages • ISBN 1-871551-54-4

In Pursuit of Lewis Carroll *by Raphael Shaberman*

Sherlock Holmes and the author uncover new evidence in their investigations into the mysterious life and writing of Lewis Carroll. They examine published works by Carroll that have been overlooked by previous commentators. A newly discovered poem, almost certainly by Carroll, is published here.

Amongst many aspects of Carroll's highly complex personality, this book explores his relationship with his parents, numerous child friends, and the formidable Mrs Liddell, mother of the immortal Alice. Raphael Shaberman was a founder member of the Lewis Carroll Society and a teacher of autistic children.

1994 • 118 pages • illustrated • ISBN 1-871551-13-7

Liar! Liar!: Jack Kerouac – Novelist *by R.J. Ellis*

The fullest study of Jack Kerouac's fiction to date. It is the first book to devote an individual chapter to every one of his novels. *On the Road*, *Visions of Cody* and *The Subterraneans* are reread in-depth, in a new and exciting way. *Visions of Gerard* and *Doctor Sax* are also strikingly reinterpreted, as are other daringly innovative writings, like 'The Railroad Earth' and his "try at a spontaneous *Finnegans Wake*" – *Old Angel Midnight*. Neglected writings, such as *Tristessa* and *Big Sur*, are also analysed, alongside better-known novels such as *Dharma Bums* and *Desolation Angels*.

R.J. Ellis is Senior Lecturer in English at Nottingham Trent University.

1999 • 295 pages • ISBN 1-871551-53-6

Musical Offering *by Yolanthe Leigh*

In a series of vivid sketches, anecdotes and reflections, Yolanthe Leigh tells the story of her growing up in the Poland of the 1930s and the Second World War. These are poignant episodes of a child's first encounters with both the enchantments and the cruelties of the world; and from a later time, stark memories of the brutality of the Nazi invasion, and the hardships of student life in Warsaw under the Occupation. But most of all this is a record of inward development; passages of remarkable intensity and simplicity describe the girl's response to religion, to music, and to her discovery of philosophy.

Yolanthe Leigh was formerly a Lecturer in Philosophy at Reading University.

2000 • 57 pages • ISBN: 1-871551-46-3

Norman Cameron *by Warren Hope*
Norman Cameron's poetry was admired by W.H. Auden, celebrated by Dylan Thomas and valued by Robert Graves. He was described by Martin Seymour-Smith as, "one of ... the most rewarding and pure poets of his generation ..." and is at last given a full length biography. This eminently sociable man, who had periods of darkness and despair, wrote little poetry by comparison with others of his time, but always of a consistently high quality – imaginative and profound.
2000 • 221 pages • illustrated • ISBN 1-871551-05-6

Poetry in Exile *by Michael Murphy*
"Michael Murphy discriminates the forms of exile and expatriation with the shrewdness of the cultural historian, the acuity of the literary critic, and the subtlety of a poet alert to the ways language and poetic form embody the precise contours of experience. His accounts of Auden, Brodsky and Szirtes not only cast much new light on the work of these complex and rewarding poets, but are themselves a pleasure to read." *Stan Smith, Research Professor in Literary Studies, Nottingham Trent University*
"In this brilliant book Murphy strives to get at the essence of 'poetry in exile' itself and to explain how it is at the centre of the whole political and cultural experience of the turbulent 20th century. His critical insight makes it one of the most important recent books on poetry in English." *Bernard O'Donoghue, Wadham College, Oxford*
Michael teaches English Literature at Liverpool Hope University College.
2004 • 268 pages • ISBN 1-871551-76-5

BUSINESS

English Language Skills *by Vera Hughes*
If you want to be sure, (as a student, or in your business or personal life), that your written English is correct, this book is for you. Vera Hughes' aim is to help you remember the basic rules of spelling, grammar and punctuation. 'Noun', 'verb', 'subject', 'object' and 'adjective' are the only technical terms used. The book teaches the clear, accurate English required by the business and office world. It coaches acceptable current usage and makes the rules easier to remember.
Vera Hughes was a civil servant and is a trainer and author of training manuals.
2002 • 142 pages • ISBN 1-871551-60-9